I CAN READ ABOUT
FOOTBALL

Written by Richard Harris
Illustrated by John Milligan

Troll Associates

Copyright © 1977 by Troll Associates
All rights reserved. No part of this book may be used or reproduced
in any manner whatsoever without written permission from the publisher.
Printed in the United States of America. Troll Associates, Mahwah, N. J.
Library of Congress Catalog Card Number: 76-54398
ISBN 0-89375-033-6

One cool, clear day in autumn, the air is filled with excitement as the first football game of the season begins.

You might be a fan. Your brother or your sister might be playing. You might be watching your very first game!

Or, you might be a player, waiting on the sidelines to get into the action.

Football is an exciting, action-packed game. It is even more exciting when you understand what's happening on the field. Here are some football words and terms that may help you . . .

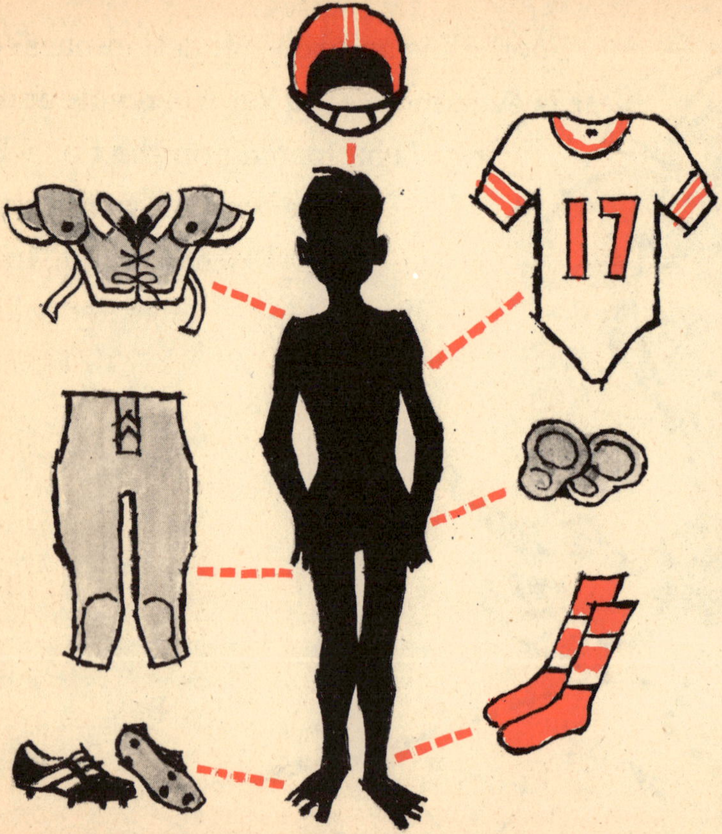

EQUIPMENT:

Some of the things a player wears are: a helmet, pants, a jersey shirt, shoulder pads, hip pads, socks, and special shoes. An important piece of equipment is the football—sometimes called the "pigskin."

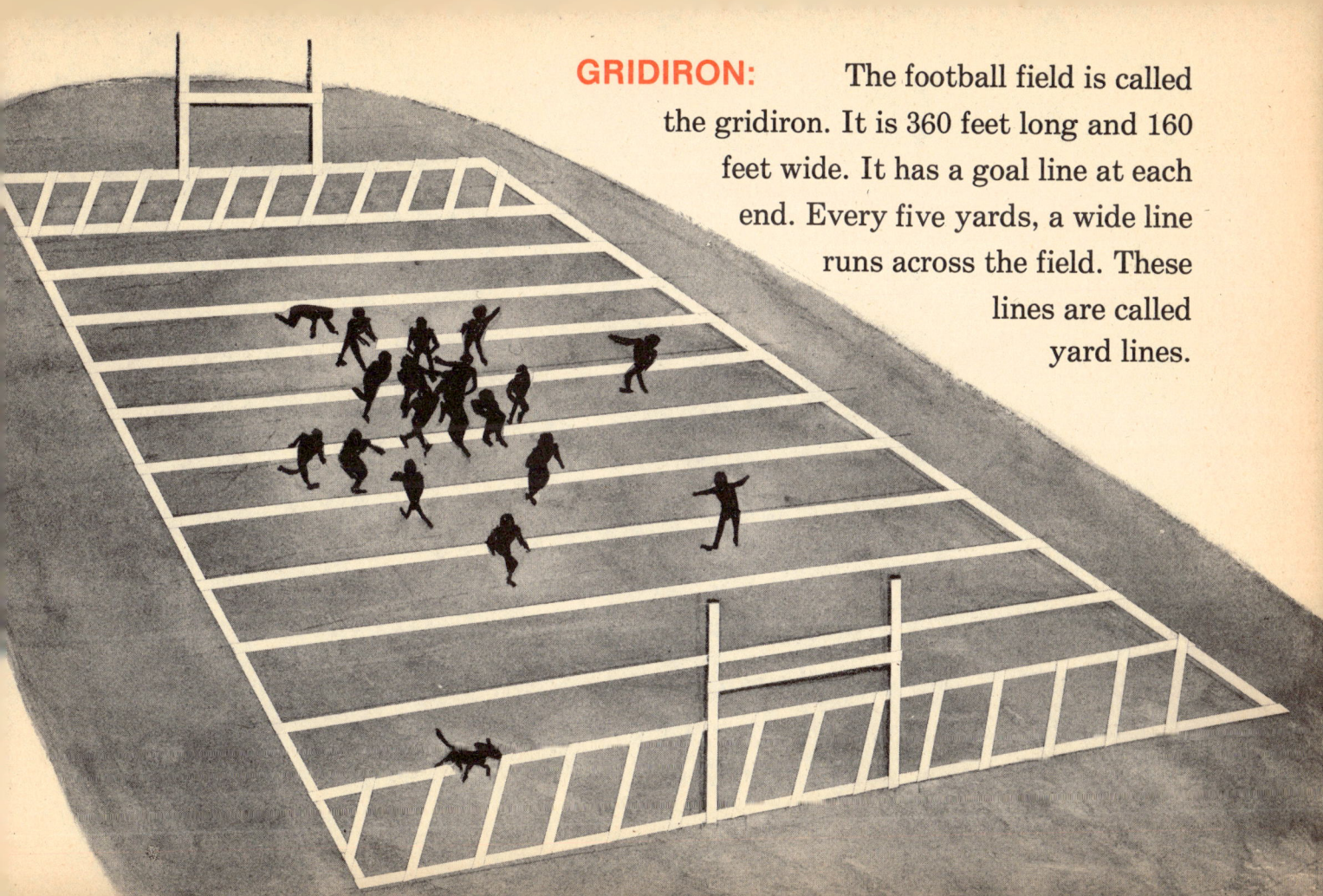

GRIDIRON: The football field is called the gridiron. It is 360 feet long and 160 feet wide. It has a goal line at each end. Every five yards, a wide line runs across the field. These lines are called yard lines.

END ZONE: The area behind the goal line is called the end zone. A player is very happy when he carries the football into the end zone. It means that he has crossed the goal line, and scored points for his team. He has scored six points!

SQUAD: The squad is the team. There are usually eleven players on the field: a quarterback, three running backs, two ends, two tackles, two guards, and a center.

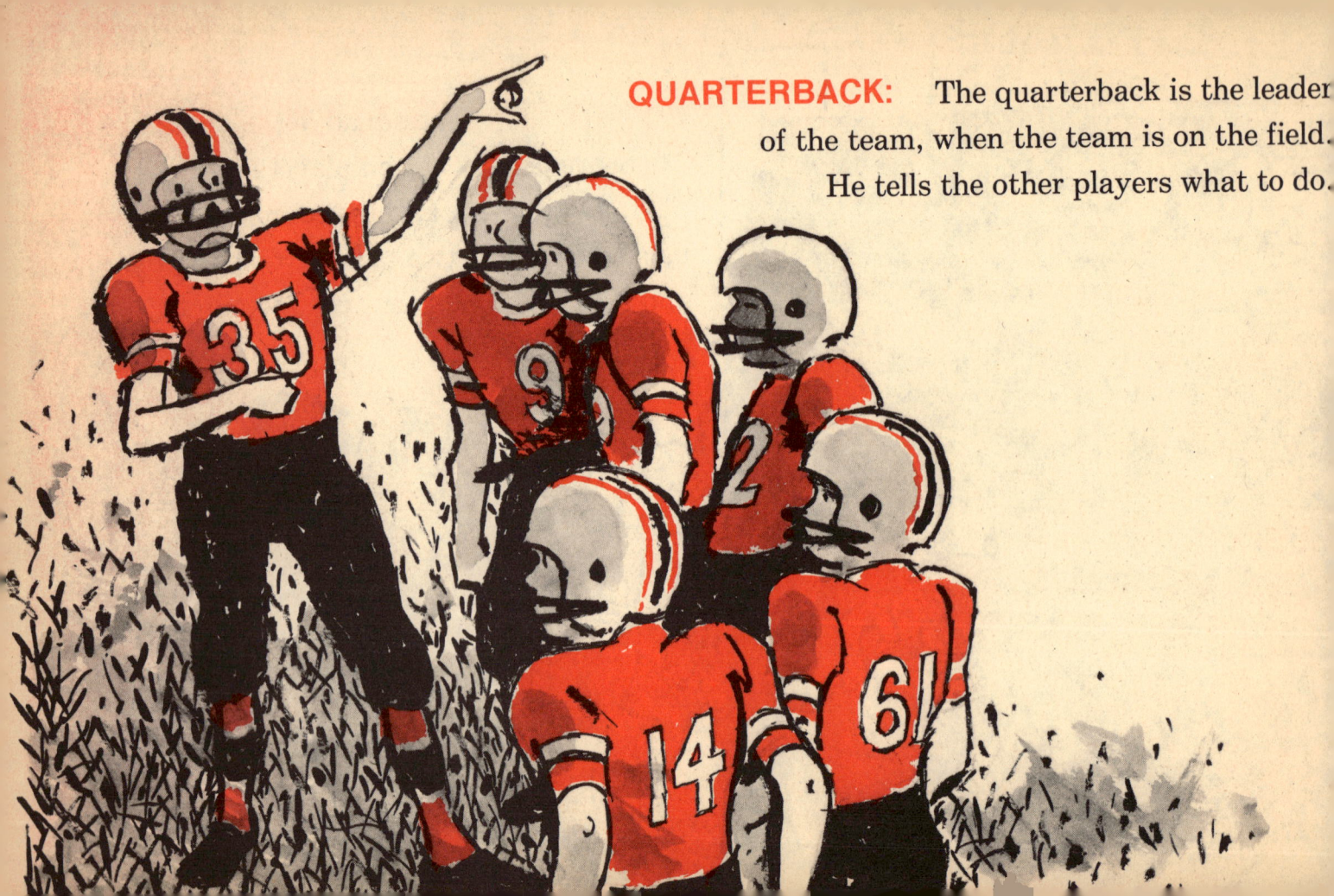

QUARTERBACK: The quarterback is the leader of the team, when the team is on the field. He tells the other players what to do.

FORWARD LINE: The ends, the tackles, the guards, and the center play on the forward line. They play *in front* of the quarterback. The players on the forward line are usually the biggest, the roughest, and the toughest players on the team.

BACKFIELD: The quarterback and the running backs play in the backfield. They play *behind* the forward line. The players in the backfield must be fast runners. It is their job to run with the ball and try to make touchdowns for the team.

TOUCHDOWN: A touchdown is made when one team carries the football over the other team's goal line. One touchdown equals six points. A touchdown is also called a "TD."

KICKOFF:

The kickoff starts the game. The football is placed near the middle of the field. One team kicks the ball to the other team.

OFFENSE and DEFENSE: When your team has the ball, you are playing offense. You are trying to score a touchdown. When your team does not have the ball, you are playing defense. You are trying to keep the other team from scoring.

LINE OF SCRIMMAGE: That's an imaginary line on the football field. It's where the ball is put into play. On each play, the team with the ball tries to get *past* the line of scrimmage to the goal line.

FIRST DOWN AND TEN YARDS TO GO: Each team gets four chances or "downs" to move the ball forward ten yards on the field. If you make it, you get a *first down*.

As long as you keep getting your ten yards, you get to keep the ball. If you don't make it, the other team gets the ball.

PUNT:

A punt is a long kick. It's best to punt when you can't make the ten yards needed for your first down.

FIELD GOAL:
On the fourth down, instead of trying for a touchdown, pro teams try to kick field goals. A field goal is kicked between goal posts. One field goal equals three points, and that's better than nothing!

HUDDLE: The team with the ball meets in a huddle. In the huddle, the quarterback calls the plays. He tells the players what to do. The quarterback speaks in a low voice so the other team cannot hear him.

SIGNALS: The quarterback calls the signals. The signals are a secret code which reminds the players what to do. Signals sometimes sound like this: "Ready, set . . . *GREEN* on two, hut one, hut two . . . *HIKE!*"

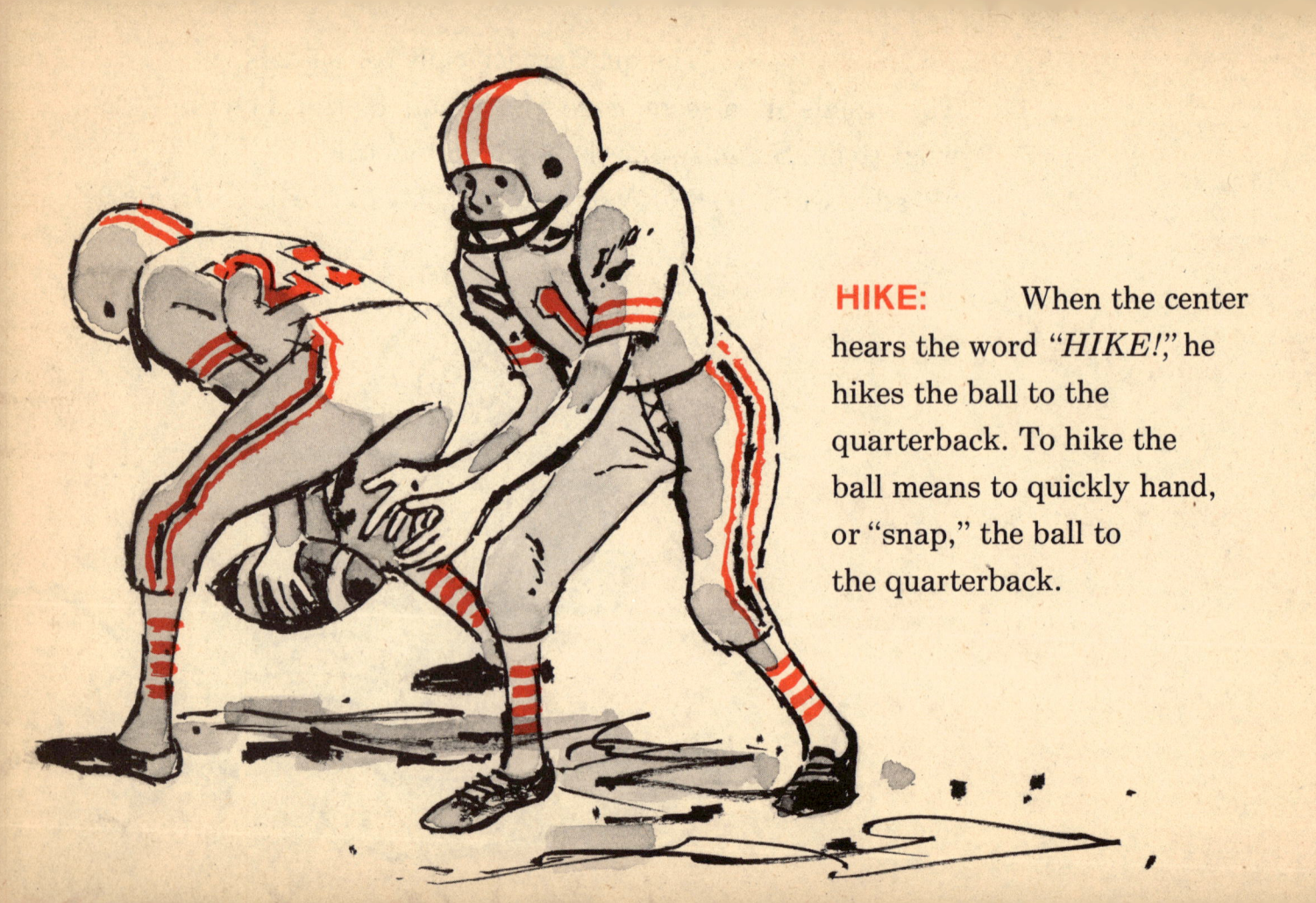

HIKE: When the center hears the word *"HIKE!,"* he hikes the ball to the quarterback. To hike the ball means to quickly hand, or "snap," the ball to the quarterback.

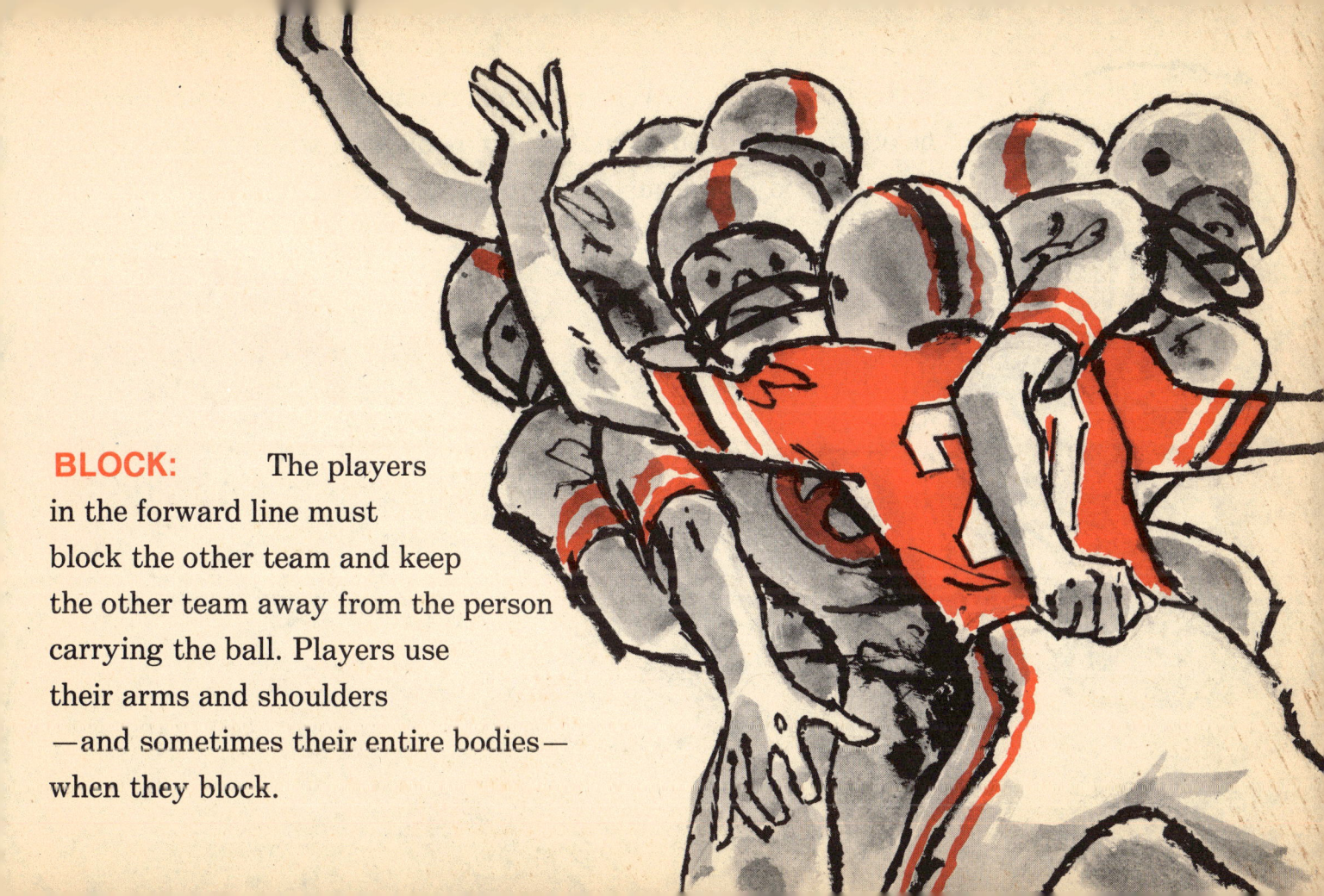

BLOCK: The players in the forward line must block the other team and keep the other team away from the person carrying the ball. Players use their arms and shoulders —and sometimes their entire bodies— when they block.

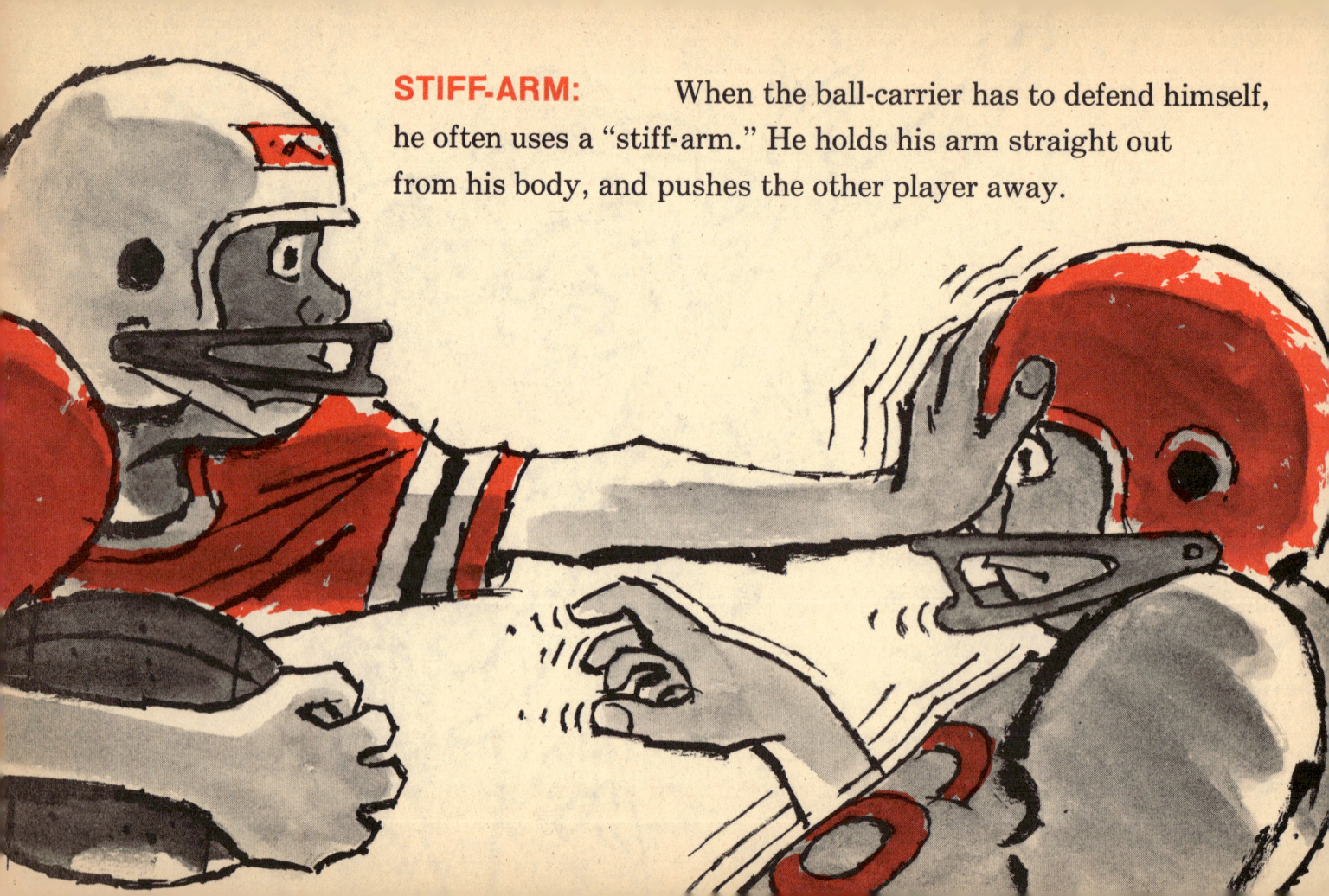

TACKLE: Very often, the other team gets past the blockers. Then, the ball-carrier has to watch out. He might be tackled. *OOMPH! THUD!*

PASS: The quarterback tries to get rid of the football before he is tackled. He passes or throws the ball through the air to a receiver who is waiting downfield to catch the ball.

FAKE: Sometimes, the quarterback only pretends to pass the ball. This is called a fake. If the other team's players are fooled by the fake, they chase after the wrong player!

FUMBLE: A ball-carrier must hang on to the ball! If he drops it while he is running, it is called a fumble. A fumble can be picked up by the other team.

GOOD HANDS: When a player is good at catching passes, people say that the player has "good hands." A football player with good hands rarely fumbles the ball. Football is no game for a player with slippery fingers!

PITCHOUT: If the quarterback quickly tosses or pitches the ball to a player in the backfield, it is called a pitchout. If he places the ball near the player's stomach, it is called a hand-off.

RUN FOR DAYLIGHT: When you get the ball, look for clear areas on the field where you can run without being tackled. This is also called "running through the holes."

BOMB: A long, high pass that sails through the air is called a bomb. The quarterback hopes the bomb will be caught by his player running into the end zone.

BLITZ: That's when one team's players —*on the defense*—go after the other team's quarterback. For a few seconds everybody goes wild. This is also called "red-dogging."

SAFETY:
The other team is awarded a *safety* when you get tackled in your own end zone. A *safety* means two points. The other team gets the points because you made a mistake!

BENCH: When you make a mistake, you may have to "ride the bench." That means you have to sit on the bench, and think about your mistake. The bench is also a good place to rest when you're not playing.

INTERCEPTION:

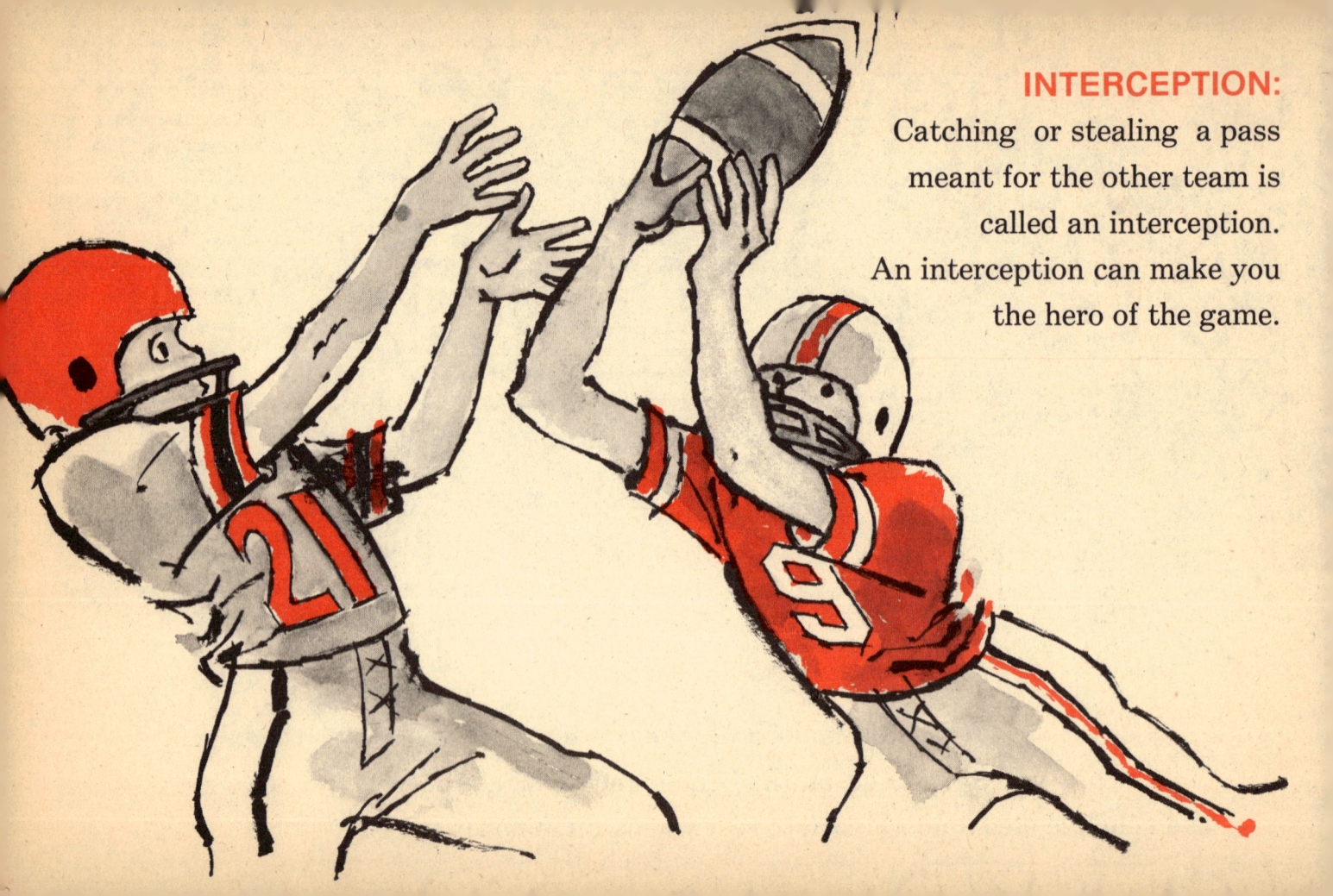

Catching or stealing a pass meant for the other team is called an interception. An interception can make you the hero of the game.

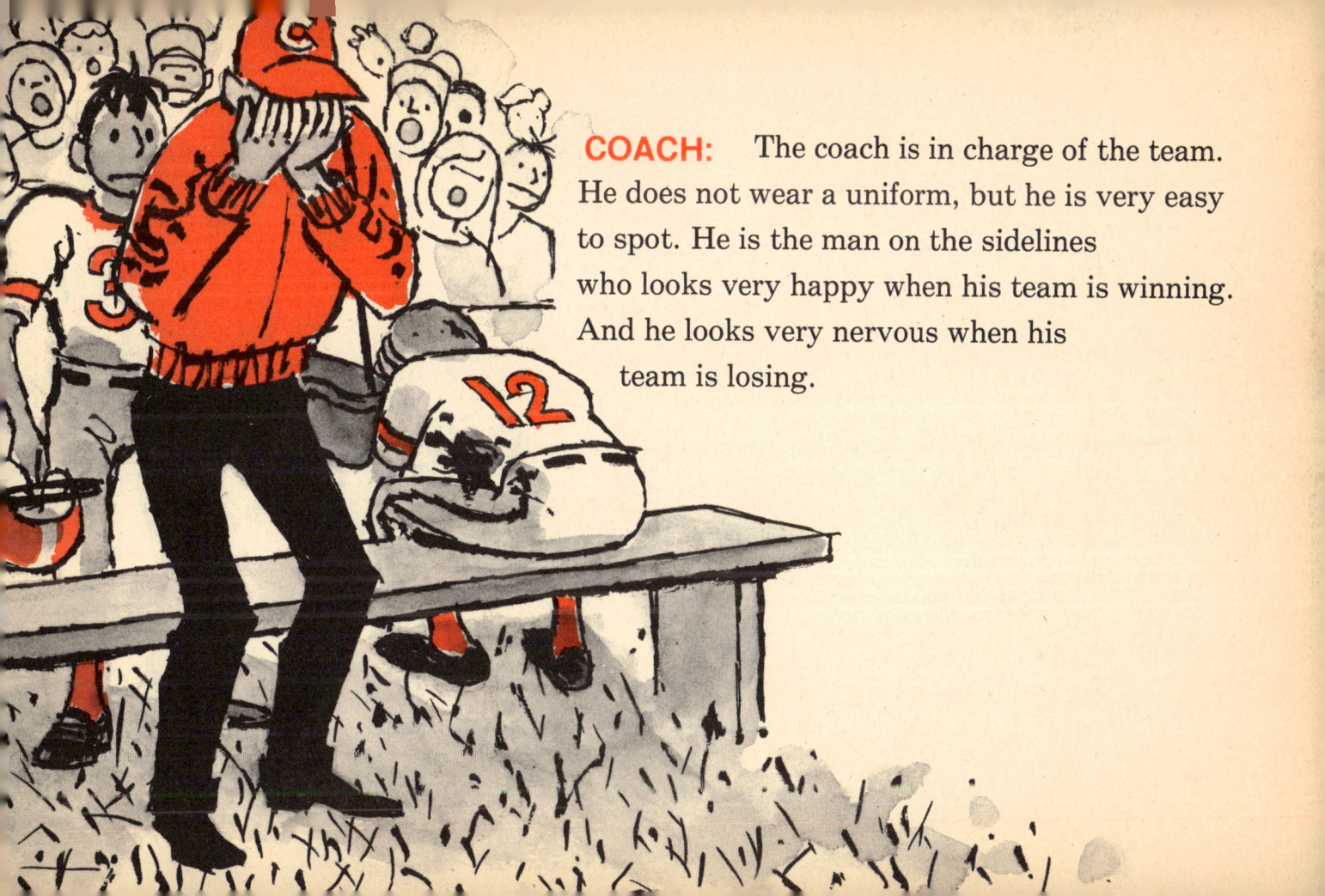

COACH: The coach is in charge of the team. He does not wear a uniform, but he is very easy to spot. He is the man on the sidelines who looks very happy when his team is winning. And he looks very nervous when his team is losing.

OFFICIALS:

Officials wear shirts with stripes, and caps. They are usually seen blowing whistles, waving their arms, and throwing flags on the field. They make sure that the players obey the rules.

PENALTY:

When an official sees a player break the rules, he calls a *penalty*. A penalty means that the ball is moved back 5, 10, or 15 yards.

FLAG ON THE PLAY:
A flag on the play means that a penalty has been called.

QUARTER: The periods of playing time in a football game are called quarters. There are four quarters in a game.

HALF TIME: Half time is a break in the game after the second quarter. It gives the players a chance to rest. Sometimes, there's a marching band to watch.

SUPER BOWL: The Super Bowl is the big game in pro football. Good college teams also play in bowl games.
In your town, your team might play for a league or conference championship.

BANG!

The gun sounds
to end the game.
The fans get ready to
leave, and your team
runs off the field cheering...
you won the game!
HOORAY!

Troll Associates